Real-Life Superpowers

PATIENCE
IS A
SUPERPOWER

by Mari Schuh

PEBBLE
a capstone imprint

Published by Pebble, an imprint of Capstone
1710 Roe Crest Drive, North Mankato, Minnesota 56003
capstonepub.com

Copyright © 2024 by Capstone. All rights reserved. No part of this publication may be reproduced in whole or in part, or stored in a retrieval system, or transmitted in any form or by any means, electronic, mechanical, photocopying, recording, or otherwise, without written permission of the publisher.

Library of Congress Cataloging-in-Publication Data is available on the Library of Congress website.
ISBN: 9780756574659 (hardcover)
ISBN: 9780756574604 (paperback)
ISBN: 9780756574611 (ebook PDF)

Summary: The line to go down the slide is so long, and you're at the back. Instead of complaining and shoving, you wait calmly. You made yet another mistake at basketball practice. You don't get upset. You keep trying. Discover more ways you can show patience and how this real-life superpower makes a big difference to those around you.

Image Credits
Alamy: Hero Images Inc., 17; Getty Images: Ariel Skelley, 5, Caia Image, 19, fstop123, 16, Halfpoint Images, 9, SolStock, 7, Shutterstock: Drazen Zigic, 15, Golden Pixels LLC, 12, Golubovy, 20 (cotton balls), Kapitosh, design element (background), MIA Studio, 13, Monkey Business Images, 11, Olga Rolenko, cover, Passakorn sakulphan, 20 (spoon), Prostock-studio, 10, Sergey Novikov, 6, XiXinXing, 8

Editorial Credits
Editor: Carrie Sheely; Designer: Bobbie Nuytten; Media Researcher: Rebekah Hubstenberger; Production Specialist: Whitney Schaefer

All internet sites appearing in back matter were available and accurate when this book was sent to press.

Table of Contents

Patience Matters...4

Patience at Home.. 10

Patience at School.. 14

Be Patient with Yourself......................... 18

Game of Patience 20

Glossary 22

Read More 23

Internet Sites 23

Index... 24

About the Author 24

Words in **bold** are in the glossary.

Patience Matters

Have you been **patient** today? What were you waiting for? Did you wait in line for lunch? Maybe you waited for the bus. How did you feel while you waited? What did you do?

Having patience means being **calm** while you wait. When people are patient, they are not upset or mad. They are **polite** and **respectful**. They are OK with waiting.

Patience is a **superpower**. Why? Things are easier to do when people are calm. Everyone is happier. They have more fun. Being patient helps make your day better. It helps people around you have a good day too.

Sometimes people forget to be patient. They want something to happen right away. They do not want to wait. When people are not patient, they can get mad and **frustrated**. Grown-ups can feel this way too!

Getting upset does not help. It does not make things go faster. It can make other people upset. It can hurt their feelings. Try to **relax** your body. Close your eyes. Take slow, deep breaths. Take a break. Then you will feel better.

Patience at Home

You can be patient at home every day. Is your sister talking on her phone? Do not **interrupt** or bother her. Wait until she is done before you talk to her.

It's time for dinner! Maybe you want to eat dessert right away. Remember to be patient. Eat your meal, then sit quietly. Wait until your family is done eating. Then you can all enjoy dessert at the same time.

Having patience helps in many ways. Jill got a new puppy. Teaching him new tricks takes time. Being patient keeps Jill and the puppy happy. It's easier to teach the puppy.

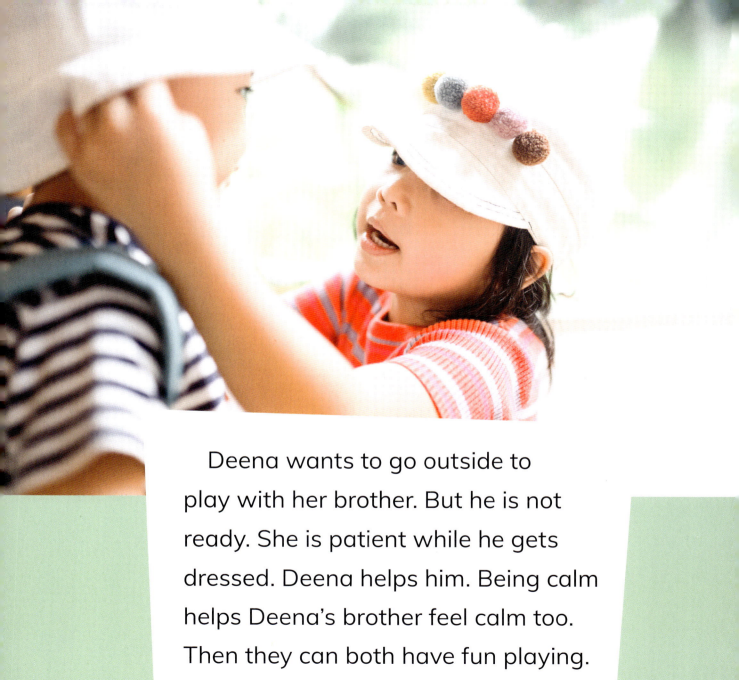

Deena wants to go outside to play with her brother. But he is not ready. She is patient while he gets dressed. Deena helps him. Being calm helps Deena's brother feel calm too. Then they can both have fun playing.

Patience at School

Being patient at school helps you be a good friend. Listen to your classmates talk before you speak. Raise your hand to answer the teacher's question. This shows you respect your classmates.

Being patient means waiting for your turn. Malik likes to go down the slide. He is patient. He does not push or yell. Malik calmly stands in line. He waits for his turn.

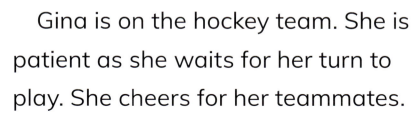

Gina is on the hockey team. She is patient as she waits for her turn to play. She cheers for her teammates.

Be Patient with Yourself

Practice being patient. Try new activities. Grow a garden. Cook with your dad. Learn to dance or play the piano. When you make a **mistake**, be patient. It takes time to learn new things.

Are you going for a long car ride? It helps to have a plan. Bring a book to read. Draw a picture. Listen to music. Then the car ride will be more fun. You will be more patient. You will be using one of your superpowers!

Game of Patience

It's helpful to practice being patient. Play this fun game as a way to be patient with yourself and others.

What You Need:

- friends
- several plastic spoons
- several cotton balls

What You Do:

1. Divide your friends into teams.

2. Choose a distance to walk for the game. It could be walking across the room and back.

3. Each team member will hold a spoon with a cotton ball on it. They need to walk for the chosen distance. If they walk too quickly, the cotton ball might fall off the spoon. Then they need to start over.

4. Players need patience to walk slowly while they hold the spoon. Patience can help a team win the game!

Glossary

calm (KAHLM)—quiet and peaceful

frustrated (FRUHS-tray-tid)—to feel discouraged and upset

interrupt (in-tuh-RUHPT)—to start talking before someone else is done talking

mistake (muh-STAKE)—something done wrong

patient (PAY-shunt)—being calm while waiting or during tough times

polite (puh-LITE)—being kind, respectful, and having good manners

relax (reh-LAKS)—to make loose

respectful (ri-SPEKT-fuhl)—believing in the quality and worth of others and yourself

superpower (soo-pur-POW-ur)—an important skill that can affect yourself and others in a big way

Read More

Emminizer, Theresa. *We Take Turns*. Buffalo, NY: PowerKids Press, 2023.

Harbo, Christopher L. *Supergirl Is Patient*. North Mankato, MN: Picture Window Books, 2019.

Rose, Emily. *Showing Patience*. Ann Arbor, MI: Cherry Lake Publishing Group, 2023.

Internet Sites

BrainPopJr.: Mindfulness
jr.brainpop.com/health/feelingsandsel/mindfulness/

Kiddle: Frustration Facts for Kids
kids.kiddle.co/Frustration

KidsHealth: What to Do When You Feel Stressed
kidshealth.org/en/kids/5-steps.html

Index

breaks, 9
breaths, 9

car rides, 18

eating, 11

interrupting, 10

listening, 14

mistakes, 18

playing, 13, 17, 18

speaking, 14

teachers, 14

teaching puppies, 12

waiting for turns, 16, 17

waiting in lines, 4, 16

About the Author

Mari Schuh's love of reading began with cereal boxes at the kitchen table. Today, she is the author of hundreds of nonfiction books for beginning readers. Mari lives in the Midwest with her husband and their sassy house rabbit. Learn more about her at marischuh.com.